DISCOVER 🐾 DOGS WITH
THE AMERICAN CANINE ASSOCIATION

I LIKE
CHIHUAHUAS!

Linda Bozzo

Published in 2017 by Enslow Publishing, LLC.
101 W. 23rd Street, Suite 240, New York, NY 10011

Library of Congress Cataloging-in-Publication Data
Names: Bozzo, Linda, author. | Bozzo, Linda. Discover dogs with the American Canine Association.
Title: I like Chihuahuas! / Linda Bozzo.
Description: New York, NY : Enslow Publishing, [2017] | Series: Discover dogs with the American Canine Association | Audience: Ages 4 and up. |Audience: K to grade 3. | Includes bibliographical references and idex.
Identifiers: LCCN 2015045443| ISBN 9780766077867 (library bound) | ISBN 9780766077997 (pbk.) | ISBN 9780766077669 (6-pack)
Subjects LCSH: Chihuahua (Dog breed)--Juvenile literature. | Dog
 breeds--Juvenile literature.
Classification: LCC SF429.C45 B69 2016 | DDC 636.76--dc23
LC record available at http://lccn.loc.gov/2015045443

Printed in Malaysia

To Our Readers: We have done our best to make sure all website addresses in this book were active and appropriate when we went to press. However, the author and the publisher have no control over and assume no liability for the material available on those websites or on any websites they may link to. Any comments or suggestions can be sent by e-mail to customerservice@enslow.com.

Enslow Publishing
101 W. 23rd Street
Suite 240
New York, NY 10011
USA
enslow.com

CONTENTS

IS A CHIHUAHUA RIGHT FOR YOU?

Chihuahuas are very small and **fragile**. They are great for families with small homes. They are loving and sweet animals.

A DOG OR A PUPPY?

Training and setting rules for a young Chihuahua should be done early. If you do not have time to train a puppy, an older Chihuahua may be better for your family.

FAST FACT:
Chihuahuas are fragile so they are better for families with older children.

LOVING YOUR CHIHUAHUA

Spend time playing with this playful pooch. You will find much to love about this small dog.

FAST FACT:
A dog harness will help protect this small dog's neck and keep it from slipping out of its collar when on a leash.

EXERCISE

Chihuahuas enjoy daily walks using a properly fitting **harness** and a **leash**. Chihuahuas also love to play indoor games, like **fetch**.

FEEDING YOUR CHIHUAHUA

Chihuahuas need only a small amount of food. Dogs can be fed wet or dry dog food. Ask a **veterinarian** (vet), a doctor for animals, which food is best for your dog and how much to feed her.

Give your Chihuahua fresh, clean water every day.

Remember to keep your dog's food and water dishes clean. Dirty dishes can make a dog sick.

Do not feed your dog people food.
It can make her sick.

Your new dog will need:

a collar with a tag

a bed

a brush

food and water dishes

a leash

toys

GROOMING

Chihuahuas will **shed**, which means their hair will fall out. Chihuahuas should be brushed once a week.

Bathe your dog when needed. A Chihauhua's nails will need to be clipped often. A vet or **groomer** can show you how. Your dog's ears should be cleaned, and their teeth should be brushed by an adult.

FAST FACT: Use a gentle soap made just for dogs.

WHAT YOU SHOULD KNOW

Chihuahuas make good watchdogs. These brave little dogs will bark at strangers.

Chihuahuas are good with cats and other Chihuahuas. They are not good with other dog breeds.

Chihuahuas are not cold-weather dogs. They do best in warmer weather.

FAST FACT:
Chihuahuas are the world's smallest dog breed.

You will need to take your new dog to the vet for a checkup. He will need shots, called vaccinations, and yearly checkups to keep him healthy. If you think your dog may be sick, call your vet.

A GOOD FRIEND

Chihuahuas can live up to 18 years. They love to be carried around. Pet and cuddle your Chihuahua. He will be a good friend to you for many years.

NOTE TO PARENTS

It is important to consider having your dog spayed or neutered when the dog is young. Spaying and neutering are operations that prevent unwanted puppies and can help improve the overall health of your dog.

It is also a good idea to microchip your dog, in case he or she gets lost. A vet will implant a painless microchip under the skin, which can then be scanned at a vet's office or animal shelter to look up your information on a national database.

Some towns require licenses for dogs, so be sure to check with your town clerk.

For more information, speak with a vet.

There are many dogs, young and old, waiting to be adopted from animal shelters and rescue groups.

fetch – To go after a toy and bring it back.

fragile – Easily hurt.

groomer – A person who bathes and brushes dogs.

harness – A piece of equipment that goes around a dog's body and is attached to the leash.

leash – A chain or strap that attaches to the dog's collar or harness.

shed – When dog hair falls out so new hair can grow.

vaccinations – Shots that dogs need to stay healthy.

veterinarian (vet) – A doctor for animals.

Books

Payne, Susan F. *The Chihuahua.* New York, NY: Kennel Club Books, LLC, 2014.

Shores, Erika. *All About Chihuahuas.* North Mankato, MN: Capstone Press. 2012.

Websites

American Canine Association Inc., Kids Corner
acakids.com/

National Geographic for Kids, Pet Central
kids.nationalgeographic.com/explore/pet-central/

PBS Kids, Dog Games
pbskids.org/games/dog/

INDEX